To

_____

From

_____

Date

_____

"I touch the future.
I teach."
—Christa McAuliffe

A Gift Book for Teachers
and Those Who Wish to Celebrate Them

What If There Were
No Teachers?

Caron Chandler Loveless
Illustrations by Dennis Hill

 HOWARD BOOKS
A DIVISION OF SIMON & SCHUSTER
New York   London   Toronto   Sydney

What if there were no teachers around?

Like, suddenly, poof! Not one could be found!

At first we might think
they must all be on break,
Just lounging and snacking
on warm coffee cake.

But after a time,
when they failed to appear,
some kid would yell out,
"Hey, what's happening here?"
There'd be chaos
and bedlam,
upheaval times three,
if teachers weren't where
we thought they should be.

The news might report,
"All teachers on strike!"
presuming they up and all took a hike.

"More money for teachers!"
the paper would say.
Even though teachers don't teach
for the pay.

At first no homework
would seem pretty cool,
and sleeping in late—
well, sure, 'cause
NO SCHOOL!

But kids would get lazy with nothing to do.
Someone must teach them, we'd say,
but just who?

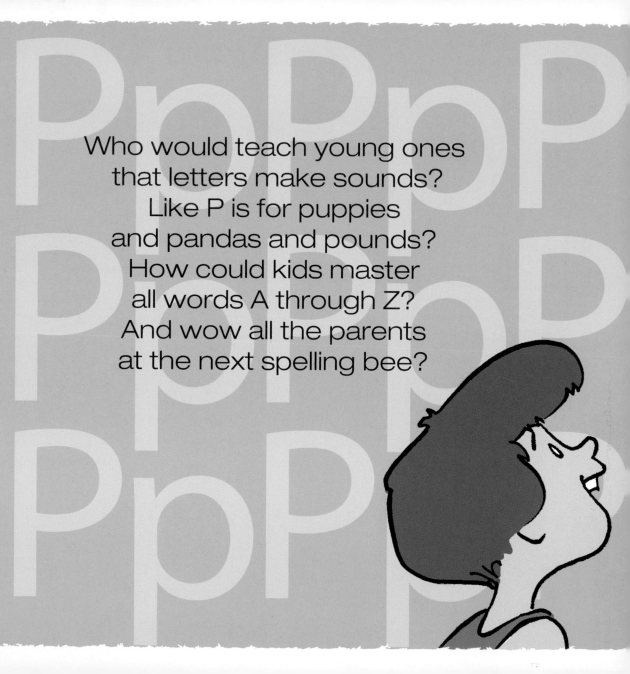

Who would teach young ones
that letters make sounds?
Like P is for puppies
and pandas and pounds?
How could kids master
all words A through Z?
And wow all the parents
at the next spelling bee?

C. 53
x 20

And then, about numbers—
well, you do the math.
The way to work fractions,
we'd all miss the path.
It would lead to more problems,
it's easy to see,
from balancing checkbooks
to a doctor's degree.

K. 25
x 18

Without language teachers,
world trade might halt.
Shops ordering sea bass
might end up with salt.
What student could learn,
"Parlez-vous français?"
And forget learning Latin,
there'd be just no way.

At lunchtime, you know just how it would go.
Spaghetti and meatballs
make great things to throw.

We'd see oodles of noodles
go splat on the wall.
Plates become frisbees in this free-for-all.

Disaster would strike
the chemistry class.
All new discoveries
would be things of the past.

Who would train doctors
to research disease?
Or which pill to give
when we start to sneeze?

Fun all-day field trips might not come to be.
Ancient rare treasures we'd all fail to see.

Without teachers teaching
we'd lose our perspective.
Attempts at great art would
turn out defective.

Who would stick papers
with smilies and stars?
Who'd say to each child,
"You're smart, yes you are!"
"Improved." "Super job!"
"That's a very good try."
Encouraging words?
You can kiss them good-bye.

Should geography class
take a permanent rest,
our north might go south;
our east might turn west.
We'd all wind up lost wherever we went.
Try as we might,
we'd not go where we're sent.

A life without teachers
would yield a high cost.
The keys to all knowledge
would surely be lost.

From passionate teachers we learn all we know.
Their care and support helps us to grow.

No, this world without teachers
we just can't allow.
Let's celebrate teachers! Let's honor.
Let's bow.

So I jump to my feet and I let out a shout.

You're
one teacher
this student
can't do
without!

"The teaching of the wise
is a fountain of life . . ."
—Proverbs 13:14 NIV

Teacher, I couldn't live without you because:

Ms. Millie ...

She reads to us!

She helps me paint.

She fixes things.

She puts my things in a bag.

She helps me color.

Thank you for being such a wonderful teacher.

♡ Karmen + Blake 2019

Our purpose at Howard Books is to:
• *Increase faith* in the hearts of growing Christians
• *Inspire holiness* in the lives of believers
• *Instill hope* in the hearts of struggling people everywhere
Because He's coming again!

HOWARD
BOOKS

Published by Howard Books, a division of Simon & Schuster, Inc.
1230 Avenue of the Americas, New York, NY 10020
www.howardpublishing.com

What If There Were No Teachers? © 2008 by Caron Chandler Loveless

ISBN-13: 978-1-4165-5197-3
ISBN-10:   1-4165-5197-2

20 19 18 17 16 15 14 13

HOWARD and colophon are registered trademarks of Simon & Schuster, Inc.

Manufactured in China

For information regarding special discounts for bulk purchases, please contact: Simon & Schuster Special Sales at 1-800-456-6798 or business@simonandschuster.com.

Edited by Chrys Howard
Cover design by Stephanie D. Walker
Interior design by Dennis Hill and Stephanie D. Walker
Illustrations by Dennis Hill